THE MOON
AT THE END OF
MY STREET

FRIENDS OF ALICE
- PUBLISHING -

ISABEL DEL RIO

THE MOON
AT THE END OF
MY STREET

**A COLLECTION OF
FACTUAL AND FICTIONAL
PERFORMANCE
POETRY**

FRIENDS OF ALICE PUBLISHING 2018

That silver shell we call the Moon.
Oscar Wilde
(The Picture of Dorian Gray, 1890)

To Charles

Table of Contents

the Moon and I

the Moon at the end of my street

there is a Moon
at the end of my street,
it keeps changing expression, tactics, behaviour,

a dead piece
of Earth that came loose, an outpost of sorts,
a retreat not a getaway,

standing discreetly
on the side as if
waiting for orders to arrive.

It appears to taunt me with its many
variants, some would say
it skillfully distracts me

from the fundamental,
−if there is anything at all
fundamental−,

both a giver
and a taker: a full Moon, giver of life,
it is claimed,

women inclined to be more fertile
then –as if fertility were an inclination-,
yet a new Moon

is nothing but a taker, its vanishing
from the skies makes us want
to disappear too, some

go all the way, according to bleak statistics, and
choose to leave
this drifting planet exactly then.

The Moon is the one thing
we share in equal measure, it
belongs to each one of us, all entitled

to a segment of the same size. And if
you do not believe this
to be true

look up and
say "My Moon!" and no
one will dispute your rights.

Yes, this is your Moon, the one commanding the
tides, the one revolving around us as if
we were its brightest star.

Lightheaded we are
from its constant spinning, its startling
moonlight, the regularity

it brings to our irregular, jagged lives,
witnesses as we are

to its monthly disappearing act.

You might be able to reach some kind of intimacy
with the Moon, and any such closeness allows
you to ask questions, though not

necessarily the right ones:
why is the Moon considered so inspiring
when it is but

one large boulder, why
play second fiddle when
it can boast craters and crevices

of its own,
why a satellite and not
a planet.

But issues such as these,
to which there is no valid answer,
might make you

lose sight
of what the Moon has allowed you
to achieve:

you promised to get
the Moon
at whatever the cost.

And that, more than anything
on the planet, is what
keeps you going, yearning.

Oh, the sweet reverie of reaching out to the Moon:
it must be the effect of the rays on
your eyes, its lack of permanence on your mind.

But I will say just this:
dream about it, yes, allow it to drive you, yes,
but do not overestimate it, this lifeless sphere

on which we have pinned our hopes,
especially when it is visible at the end of your street
on certain days of the month.

seas

who would not want to be on the Moon
when its has
so many seas,
made from our very own dust and with
names that I can only
dream of:

the sea of nectar
sea of serenity
sea of foam
sea of vapours
sea of fecundity and sea of cleverness
sea of moisture
sea of humour
sea of clouds
even a lake of sleep

and only upon the sea of tranquility did Apollo astronauts
walk

my darker side

my dark side as that of the Moon,
never stepped
upon,
no giant leaps for
anyone to call the shots,

too far away
to bother about exploration.
Or could it be that with one small step
you are in, right
inside the darkest of the dark, for it is not

as far away as you had
anticipated?
Like the Moon, I am drifting
away from Earth, the only
certainty

I have for now,
but then where
am I going about my business
like the Moon, travelling through space at 1.3 million miles an
hour?

I cannot but think about
my 68 per cent of dark
energy, my 27 per cent of dark matter, and
like the Moon, I am
sometimes visible,

and other times imperceptible,
yet renewed month after month. Oh Moon, you
who attracts and repels,
let your rays lighten
my nights, refresh my days, to thee I pray, I sing,

together we will
discover our darkest side,
and confirm that there is nothing to it, the Moon's
or mine, except that light
never shone on it blindingly before.

hands and lips

Look at my hands, not aging hands yet,
but you can feel a draught in the crooks and
a barrenness in the mounds,
they are more angular than they once were.

And now look at my lips, finer than
before, not a blossom
but a leaf, not a full protruding pout but
a lanky pointed grin.

not a dazzling life-giving star, but a dead, obedient Moon, so
to speak.

And yet this is me, even now it is me.
Inside I do not feel my lips
and hands are fast fading into
stupor.

Inside I feel the same as ever, and
I can only ask whether it will still
be like this once these hands are reduced
to bone, these lips to ash.

Will it come gradually that desecration of the body, so to
speak,

by demise itself,
or will it be slow so
to allow us
to get used to

its new
melodramatic state?
Or lack of
state, as it were?

These hands to hold will hold nothing perhaps soon
enough, so to speak,

these lips to say those words of love and
kiss the face
of love will find
unsolicited

rest to their constant
repositioning,
their never-ending talking,
kissing, tasting.

All that and more is to be deciphered in the end, so to speak,

but who will we then
tell
the story to?
There will be no one to

converse with,
nowhere
to come
back from,

I look at my hands and already see them as skeletal and slight,
so to speak,

I lick
my lips and I can
already feel the
dust that they

will one day
become, a far away,
darkened planet
with no moons.

I am also Death, my own birth, the future as sand or stone, the
endless goings on of a plan or possibly a plot, so to speak

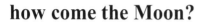

how come the Moon?

duets

new Moon,
comes too soon

waxing crescent,
not truly present

first quarter,
bricks and mortar

waxing gibbous,
one more quiver

full Moon,
a bright lagoon

waning gibbous,
of this rid us

last quarter,
getting shorter

waning crescent,
evanescent

legacy

on a copper disk –gold-plated 14-inch phonograph
record– you will find everything
you ever wanted to leave behind when you are no longer

here. A time capsule from the planet Earth sent
to outer space on Voyager, back in 77, will explain to
future generations what we once were, should

we disappear soon enough
with all the tribulations distressing the planet, it might be one
way of surviving, in name only, of course,

and so
this copper disk
will be left behind to symbolize

what we once did, who we once were, millennia
of civilization reduced to a few examples of human
achievement, a handful of accomplishments here and

there. And if it is the case that we should disappear
into oblivion soon enough, this will be
the only artefact left by us

in the whole of this expansive universe, not only
as we know it, but as we
do not,

for at the time the disk was created
all these depicted objects were considered
the most instructive or the most beautiful, or both,

to leave behind, but then what
will space-drifting extra-terrestrial
civilizations

think of us when, in 40,000 years, the Voyager
craft will get close enough to
another planetary system, and they –if

there is anyone out there, for
we might be alone in this
vast expanse of space–, will check us

out, discuss our fate, probably laugh (if that is something
they are capable of), for such a disk will contain engraved
in its bright copper grooves all of the following:

one hundred and
fifteen
images

including various anatomical views, a seashore,
sand dunes, fallen leaves, as well as
Andean

girls, a dancer
from Bali, a grape picker, a nursing mother, sunset with

birds, Golden Gate

Bridge, the UN building, a Chinese dinner
party, a snowflake
over Sequoia, a *Xancidae* seashell, a calibration

circle, a diagramme
of a foetus, a family
portrait, a tree surrounded by daffodils, Jane

Goodall and chimps, elephant,
crocodile, old man with beard, old
man with dog, children, schoolroom, airplane,

airport, page of Newton's
Philosophiæ Naturalis Principia Mathematica, radio
telescope, train,
factory, museum, fishing

boat, underwater scene, mountain climber,
gymnast, craftsman, people
cooking

fish in Spain, licking,
eating,
drinking, interior

of a house,
a forest, a fertilized
ovum, sex

organs, mathematical definitions,
physical unit
definitions, flying insect, school of fish,

a cautious diagram
of conception, a rush-hour scene,
a woman with

a microscope, street scene in Pakistan, Antarctic
expedition, highway, the city of Boston,
the city of

Oxford, the Taj Mahal, the Great Wall
of China, Amish country,
and then

all those sounds, natural sounds, as those made by surf, wind,
thunder and animals like birds
and whales, a hyena, the kiss of a mother,

the sound of a tractor, a bus, a tame
dog, a volcano,
thunder, an earthquake,

music by Bach, Mozart, Beethoven, Stravinsky,
Guan Pinghu, Blind Willie Johnson, Chuck
Berry, Kesarbai Kerkar, Valya Balkanska,

especifically the Well-Tempered Clavier, the Queen
of the Night aria no. 14, Johnny B. Goode, aborigine
song "Morning Star", Navajo

song "Night Chant", section from Partita
No. 3, Melancholy
Blues by Louis Armstrong,

verbal greetings in 55 languages, beginning with

Akkadian, spoken in Sumer 6,000 years ago, and ending
with a modern Chinese dialect, Wu,

and also printed messages from the then U.S.
president Jimmy
Carter and the then

UN Secretary-General Kurt
Waldheim (yes, sadly, he who tried to hide
his complicity in Nazi crimes),

the inspirational message
Per aspera ad astra ("Through hardship to
the stars") in Morse code,

and further images, this time of food, architecture, humans
depicted in portraits but also doing the things we all
normally do or try to do, shopping

in a supermarket, nursing
a baby, working in
a factory,

and then the final legacy, yet the most unreliable
piece of evidence: a recording
of Anne Druyan's brainwaves

when trying to explain
what it is like to fall
in love,

and all this may be discovered in a distant and detached
future, but it may also be lost in space, in the same way
as we are now, mostly, lost

in the midst of space. And therefore the gist of the story
of what we have achieved until now,
as you can see, does not amount to much, just a 14-inch

phonograph disk, and yet
we have filled continents and
millennia with history and events, we

have traced our ancestors all the way to the first living cell,
have imagined
the future into the vast space where Voyager

has been
travelling for four decades now, and
who knows if one day

we will receive something similar
from far away, a copper disk, a gold-plated
14-inch phonograph record where

we will find what someone somewhere
wanted to leave behind when they were no longer
here, perhaps

with hundreds of images, sounds, music, voices and
greetings, with the sound of the
wind and of birds, with

the fastidious anatomy of sex and
the unmistakable
brainwaves of love,

but when it reaches us, it will be too late

to redeem those who sent it, given the vast distances,
the even vaster incomprehension, and the question

to ask is whether it will also be too late to redeem us, in
this our solitary confinement, in our planet
of planets, alone with our own images and sounds.

Perhaps it is all an experiment of some sort,
a way of calling out, a flicker
that is put out sooner than expected.

And in all this concoction, I forgot to mention
that image number 115 includes the planets
of our solar system, the Moon of our Earth

four hundred times

the symmetry of a total solar eclipse
happens
because, by perfect chance,
the Sun is four hundred times larger than
the Moon,
but it is also four hundred times
remoter
from the Earth, and this
simple coincidence
makes these two bodies, Sun and
Moon, stellar bodies so meaningful to us (for our lives
rotate around them, in more ways than one)
that they appear as
having exactly the same size
on the sky,
one covering the other
flawlessly during such an eclipse, and so
my advice is that, if
you are going to create a
coincidence, make
it as mind-blowing as this one

occultation

in 357 B.C.
Aristotle recorded the Moon covering

Mars,

a mere satellite
concealing the belligerent

planet,

showing off that it can
get away with it:

"Why,

I can stand in the way, and leave Mars
out of the picture!"

 Satellite

where anything denting it
survives

forever

or at least for ten million years because
there is no

wind

and no motion, a rocky,
cratered

landscape,

almost perfectly preserved, as it was
when created 4.5 billion years ago, no

atmosphere,

no air, on this side
crevices of hardened

magma,

whereas the far side is a
smoother, gentler

body,

unmoved by all the fuss we make
about it, it hides

half

of itself
from view, as if inadmissible

evidence,

something conveniently close, so we can explore it
to find that out that it is just a

 relic,

but fittingly far away so that we can call it what we want,
even

History.

And thus it will remain, for our sake
and in our defence, in total

silence

the Moon and you

exploring

dedicated to RF

Mangled fingers touch me, tips missing,
no nails. Crotch with funny side burns, not
the fruit of love but the infection of old. Eyelids
droopy, not the fruit of age but the child of
ice burn. Lips

like pebbles warmed up on the seafront. Skin
like hide, the sharpest teeth. Not
so much man
but mostly animal, since the only thing
on his mind for so long

has been survival. He
has an urge not for love but, if you can call
it that, interfacing with everything in his path. What
is worse is that he has been alone in the vast
expanse of the

Arctic, at times not knowing how much further
there was to go. A distance
as immense as the mind or outer space?
Perhaps he was never aware of how
far he had travelled,

and instead thought it was
a different realm, the kingdom
of the
unexplored, and more so
the unresolved.

Back then, the compass worked
and could not
lie, but magnetism both
attracts and
repels, the

closer to the Pole the further from
the truth. Was
that not the reason he went there?
To flee from what he thought was true and right? To hide
and be nothing, to get

unreservedly lost? Or was it to avoid
being found? Had
he not sent the signal
when rot set in, or when a stone
shot down his kidney, or

when frostbite hit him hard at his fingertips? Yes,
then he called. A simple message,
down a radio line. SOS.
Or was it
help me, for I am lost?

Was he not aware that
not all that is lost
can be found?
Rescue me!
He said those very words back then.

He must have been in awe
of all that snow pallor around him, a semblance
of eternity maybe.
"Rescue me!" I think
I heard him say

right now, but it could have been me
saying it, sooner or later we all need to be rescued. Yet
nothing was eternal
in that room where we
were. What would happen next

I would not know.
"Rescue me!"
His hair has not aged.
That is the one feature
that remains the same, abundant

and thick, even
the colour is as it must have been back then.
"Do you dye your hair?"
He jumped on the bed.
"What?"

I didn't ask the same thing again, but something more
insolent instead.
"Why did you stop exploring?"
Why did you put an end to your
endless travels through

snowstorms and blizzards, trying to prove that
Nature is something to be
subdued and not
reckoned with,
coming close to

death so many times? Is it
that you were afraid of ice itself, all that
white, black, grey, grey-white, soft,
fast, frazil, ground, bare,
brash, close, friendly,

compact, drift, grease and grounded ice?
And why did you stop
electrifying me with the tips of the
fingers that once were? Those
cut down tips

without nails, those stubs of a hand, those
five morsels of flesh that gripped
you in a handshake
like it was the end, and
were now

gentle and yet effective
on my folds of flesh.
"Do you feel anything?"
He said he didn't, but I
definitely did.

"Felt what?"
He jumped again on the bed, and
repeated the question.
"Felt what, I said?"
The same, if not more, as what you

felt in the midst of the snow-covered landscapes, the bleakest
solitude, the interminable summer days,
the sparkle of that
one long winter night, the longing
for home

and yet the unearthing of a strength within you
that pushed you to fight with Nature to the death and,
when absolutely necessary,
surrender willingly to the elements as if to fate itself. It was
frailty

and strength all in one. How inscrutable
your thoughts in the wilderness, how your bouts of
despair were followed by dreams of conquest, how
you lived with
the memory

of home and love and sex and
a woman wailing from pleasure and
yet irate because we are all selfish
and need our own pleasure
over and above the exploration of the world.

It is only then, when he had finished, that
I was able to
breathe out.
"Is that what you feel when
you're provoked?"

I would not call it a provocation but it was a word
as good as any to describe the event. And
with those stubs, non-sentient, long-lost fingers,
memories of what once had held
and caressed, he touched me gently yet decisively, as

if gripping a sledge on snow, grabbing on to
a kite to travel over ice, crushing a slab of frost, staking
a tent in the highest winds, fighting a storm
that had the might
of a thousand giants, and

I was done.
"Yes!"
"Yes, what?"
He asked, pretending
not to have noticed my wailing. Or was it

that he could not compare it to anything
he knew.
"I felt the same as you felt in the snow!"
He smiled, as if he knew
that to be the case. We were now

equals, each
with our own means of
exploration, having possibly
felt identical
sensations, with a full set of emotions similar in nature.

This was the beginning of our bond.
Or could it be the end?
And as he left, he said what
I had been expecting:
"And now I am going to the Moon!"

if we did not have the Moon

If we did not have the Moon
our days would be six hours long,
our seas would stand still,
our nights would be pitch black with a few stars
thrown in
for effect.

If we did not have the Moon
we would not sing to it or dance around it, we
would not make up prayers to allay
evil or attract blessings,
no one would think there is a man on the moon who lives
there for whatever reason, however justified.

If we did not have the Moon
we have no satellite to
keep us company along this perilous trek,
we would not know eclipses
of the Sun, of the Moon, we would not even
have made up that melodious word *eclipse*.

If we did not have the Moon
there would be no lunacy,
no one would be moonstruck,
moonrise and moonset would cease to be,
we would not be affected
by the Moon, our moods, our menstrual cycles.

If we did not have the Moon
we would not talk about
milk Moon and
rose Moon,
chrysanthemum Moon,
and ripe corn Moon,

windy Moon and panther Moon,
the Moon
when June berries are ripe,
the Moon when
quilling and beading are done, the Moon
of the terrible, the Moon

when eyes are sore from the white snow, the long
night Moon, and the open
sea Moon
Moon of horses, of wind,
of ice,
Moon of the middle summer,

singing Moon, of winds,
of awakening,
women's Moon,
the Moon when the geese
return
in scattered formation.

If we did not have the Moon
we would not know the storm moon
and the chaste moons,
the barley and the blood moons,
the oak and the hare moons,
the tree moons.

If we did not have the
Moon, there would be no full Moon
for wolves to howl at,
no vampires to wake up, no one at all
to turn into
a werewolf.

If we did not have the Moon,
we would not have moondogs or mockmoons,
we would not know what to do with
the many moons of Saturn and Jupiter,
of Uranus or Neptune,
the two moons of Mars.

If we did not have the Moon,
we would not know what to call
the night, perhaps only
darkness, we would it describe it
only by its colour, black, we would define it
by its lack of purpose, pointless.

No one would be over the Moon
When happy.
Things would not have
happened many moons ago, so possibly not at all.
No one would bother
to reach out for the Moon, to aim for it, to want it.

If we did not have the Moon
there would be no honeymoons for
lovers,
no moonscapes nor moonquakes
nor moondust,
no moonlighting.

No moonglade,
no moonflowers,
no moonstones,
no moonlight,
no moondrop,
no moonwalking.

check it out!

You said that you
had not seen the Moon because
you had never looked in that direction.

You explained that, in a way, you did not want
to find it, so that you
would never have to lose it.

Why, I asked. and you replied:
as with everything,
at the precise moment you discover

the Moon
you have to be willing
to give it up.

As if saying hello
implied a goodbye, the beginning
is really the end.

Or as they say: the moment you are born
you have to brace
yourself for your demise.

Such is the Moon,
such its detachment from us, such
is the struggle

against time. So, before it is
all up and gone, rise to the occasion and check
it out!

shoot the Moon

We tried hard to invent it,
to build it on Earth and send it into orbit
on a powerful rocket, made
sure it rotated according to plan
and did what it
was told.

This was the official version that
everyone
believes.
It is in history books, in science
books, even in
the Constitution.

We made it possible
for someone
to own it, and so there were
shares of
the Moon, a lunar stock market,
stores selling anything

to do with it
and people buying
whatever was on offer.
In all, merchandising
bits of rock and rocks in bits
has been profitable.

We established a capital
city, a province,
a region, a country; we offered
tours of craters and seas;
we founded
the newspaper, Moon Times.

We even invented a
language with
half of the letters
visible and
the other half
hidden.

A new form of Art inspired by
moonbeams suddenly
appeared
out of nowhere,
without a single precursor in the field, possibly
without a serious future.

But Art sold
in its thousands, just like
the thousands of
bits of rock sold
in airports
and supermarkets.

We confronted the problem of
cold nights and
lack of atmosphere
by transforming
the Moon
with glass chambers where

we could breathe and
move,
its surface
no longer what it used to be,
but now one long, unreceptive
shopping mall.

We swore at it, took it for
granted, denied its
antiquity and its origins,
the truth, in one word,
for we had always thought it was a human invention, like
everything else we had been taught.

We created
enemies
out of those simply gazing
at the Moon, since
there was
now a charge.

Others desired it at a more substantial level
and fought bloodily
for it; wars broke
out, for the Moon was strategically
important
and materially viable.

And one day, to put an end to the conflict
to end all conflicts, our
Council decided that
we would switch it off: "Switch off the Moon!"
There was a vote; we all
had a ballot paper; it was after all a democracy.

Like the Moon, supposedly created on Earth, we
did what we were told.
And it all happened as planned.
They called it a lunar eclipse,
except that it would
last forever.

There was no Moon any longer,
and no more moonlight at night, no
more celestial companion. And
all those involved in the various
lunar affairs
took their business

elsewhere, for there is
always a credible way to tell a story,
always a price
to sell what nobody may
readily want.

Moon Seasons

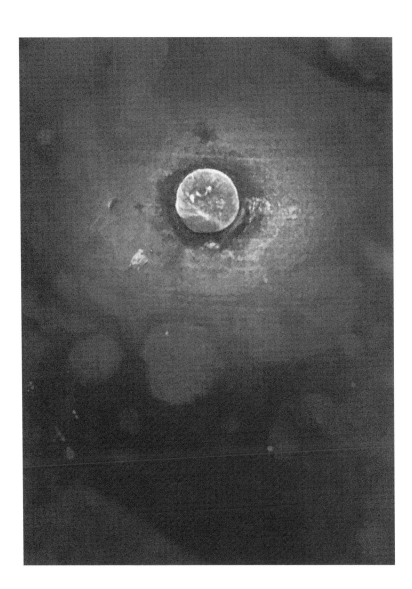

Spring Moon

flowers in Spring
imprint their identity
on everything they touch,
their perfect colours embarrassing
all other shades,
perpetually pollinating
landscapes
whilst no one else
is looking,
doubtless unafraid of performing
a sexual
act in public.
All of this is done
with such determination
that one would think those seasonal changes
were here to stay, and Spring
would rightly last forever.
But nothing, no one, can enjoy any
kind of permanence since
nothing, no one,
can endure for too long
such trials –could they be experiments?–
or such burdens
–might they be an eventual loss of interest
on our part?–

and as a consequence
the seasons
repeat themselves in perpetuity,
as
if objectively
there was no
other option but to go on
and hastily on,
in all a despicable act of self-deception.
Flowers in Spring
exude scents that pre-empt
what will be done to perpetuate
their seed, overriding
all in their path because, it would appear,
nothing, no one
else seems to matter,
sweet potions seducing
yet sneakily
driving us from lukewarm to blaze,
from seed to fruit,
from ash to procreation.
A taster, an act of impatience,
a curtain raiser,
a business card, a breeze
warning us of a greater wind, a rainy day
without having saved for it,
but at the same time
a brutal admonition
of the threat of Summer.
And despite that difference
in personality, Spring
gently hands the relay
in this race
to imminent

and summery
occurrences –blistering and
urging to burst forth–,
its pale pink colours foretelling
the scarlet of a daunting and balmy haze.
As to the Moon, it is the brightest
it will ever be.

Summer Moon

Look at us in Summer,
allowing ourselves to
be drawn in by
agonizing temperatures,
the sort that demand ad-libbing at most
times,
for there can be no preparation
for this kind of excess,
and
anything goes
in the business of trying
to defend ourselves from the
almightiest blaze, all the way
from fiercely rebelling
against what is handed down
to abiding by the rules and taking it all
in your stride.
Yes, the heat will probably awaken
passions, but it provides
no true deliverance.
Such radiance does, in some cases,
allow us to imagine how far we
might just go,
wide is the mind,

innumerable your guesses,
forever is the word to keep to yourself.
It could be that, in a warm
and welcoming setting, the right to
dream
knows no bounds
because
extreme heat brings
about the audacity to
speak out thoughts
and beliefs,
launching us into a
make-believe adventure of no return and,
better still, no regrets.
Becoming truly free (because of the heat
or in spite of it?) is
another matter, but
we are cheerfully deluded
for now.
And as time goes by,
the battlefront is plagued
by yet even more enemies (the double-edged sword
of heat, to be followed
by the wind, to be followed by
the cold), but this fact
gradually ceases to be important
and we end up convincing ourselves
that Summer is on our side.
No, no one will ever be prepared for warmth
that suffocates and
turns us into even more
outlandish creatures (is it true
that most crimes
are committed during

heatwaves?), so barely
can we resist and not capitulate.
It might be best then to forget
the fact that this, the fiercest of fires,
will soon be extinguished
and in its place,
unassuming though possibly
more ominous,
something new (and it could well provide
fresh opportunities)
would appear, a cooler
setting where the wind will blow like
it has lost its direction
and will carry away
leaves and boughs
in their hundreds,
thoughts of old
in their thousands.
The renewal that seasons bring about
could well erase those things
that are most relevant, lost as
they might be in the shuffle and exchange, and so
from season to season we forget what
once held us together, what
we aspired to and wished for
so desperately.
For your sake,
do not
allow the joy of novelty
to carry you away, you
might well lose your perspective
in the process
and forget the season you
are living in.

Look here and now, there seems
to be lurking
a new menacing season,
without
anyone realising it is
fast approaching us.
Look out, Autumn is literally
just around the corner
from where you are sitting placidly
without
thinking for one second
that there could be an end
to this scorching yet idyllic Summer.
Beware then
because, from hot to cold,
it is now a matter of days.
And this Moon is almost
as warm and radiant as the sun, or
so we like to think in
these long summer nights,
deceptively so.

Autumn Moon

In Autumn I
begin to feel that
I am running
out of time
and have been left to
my own devices, and all because
no one appears to know
what this is all about: the repetition
of the seasons, the endless dwelling
on why it happened and who
in responsible and where
we are going from here.
So many questions posed
with a backdrop of
greenery that is
now bronzed and decaying, as if
the path behind me
had ceased to be, no more footsteps
or memories or past events.
As to the path in front
of me, I dread
to think where it will lead, the *unknown*
is an accurate enough word,
although it suggests nothing at all.
So where I am going, no one can say.
A fact is the cold, a greater fact is

the irrepressibility of the cold.
To deal with such facts and comparisons
I am camouflaged, but not to
my advantage.
No more fruits to offer (by Autumn, or
by me or by both?), there is
barely a presence of what I once
lived so intensely, barely
a shadow of who I
cared to be back then.
And now, in the midst of this picture-perfect
Autumn, I have become
undergrowth, brushwood,
scrub,
fruit no more, nor bud, nor stem, nor
stalk nor shaft nor shank,
nor root, nor bush nor shrub.
Just undergrowth, do you understand?
The fact that I can speak and
think
does not allow me to have more rights
than thickets or fungi, or ivy or ferns.
And so, I make do
with fallen leaves,
and I put up with
rotten trunks.
I am happy to look at
bare trees, fields
without flowers,
gardens that have ceased to be glorious
and lush,
around me
solely thunderstorms
and blizzards

and gales,
all immobilizing me with their
chilly outlook
instead
of sunrays
warming my flesh.
And I tune my mind
to accept the undeferrable
cold, aware as I am
that it is no more
than a ploy to appease us
in preparation
for the tragic events
of an impending Winter.
As to the Moon, it is less visible now, as if
losing interest in what we
have become, or
even planning
a total retreat.

Winter Moon

We lament the predictable
outcome, the only one
there can ever be, we
have no choice,
we are running out of time,
such brief, melancholy days
they are,
wretched the plight of birds fleeing
and flowers withering.
The only delight is knowing
that shortly
a new repertory of
stems will grow, seeds of every
species will sprout,
rose petals will be born,
trees will burst out joyously
with leaves.
Some people
say they feel the cold
only in Winter; for others Winter
is all year round;
for a few it spells the underworld
itself: from the beginning,
the end was made perfectly
clear to us, no one ever deceived us, that is for sure.

In my case, the cold is but
a chance
to light bonfires, to look for
heat wherever it may be, to feel
unexplored emotions, all
the more intense
because they will end soon
enough.
We cannot help but to emulate
each season to the smallest
detail, in
parallel motions, may we be as exacting as
they are. And so,
contrary
to what this Winter is about,
my own Winter
is not followed
by seasons of any sort, there are
essentially
no flowers to blossom, no
seeds
that promise any kind of future, no fruits
to bear, there is
no more,
nothing, no one.
And despite such undeserved ending
to this whole undertaking,
from my remains
diverse dreams, conjectures
and, one would hope, occasions
will somehow sprout, and
perhaps
one day
those

brightly-coloured flowers
will bloom, exuding
painlessly
the scents of Spring.
As to our Moon,
all throughout the winter months
it is far from waning,
picking up
where it left off, and
shining almost brighter than a star.
Some would think
it is a midnight sun, a not so
convincing performance of warming up
the frozen world, a true
act of defiance
since everything
is dormant now and
about to awaken,
but not yet,
no,
not yet.

Moon haikus

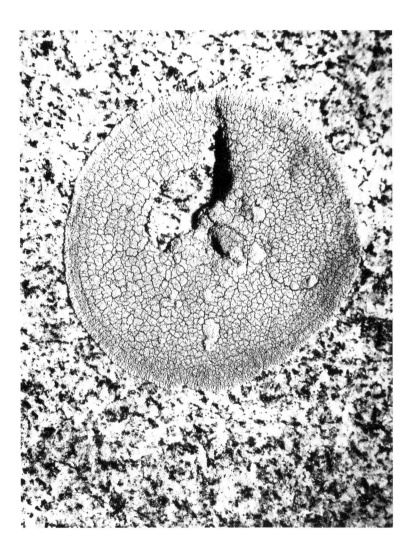

Moon Haiku Number 1

Like you, the Moon is
not in the universe, but
is the universe

Moon Haiku Number 2

a waning crescent
Moon is called an old Moon, in
the east before dawn

Moon Haiku Number 3

constant reminder
is the Moon, gentle prodding
just to comfort you

Moon Haiku Number 4

a spoiler alert
is this disk: that it all ends
sooner or later

Moon Haiku Number 5

I am here to stay
as the Moon is my witness,
yet will not be still

Moon Haiku Number 6

Look up and see what
is awaiting relentless
somewhere in the skies

Moon Haiku Number 7

I used to believe
that the Moon was the night sun
on a dim backdrop

Moon Haiku Number 8

No, nothing can come
ever between you and me,
except for the Moon

Moon Haiku Number 9

Is it an eye or
an ear, the mouth or the nose
of the universe?

Moon Haiku Number 10

When all is said and
done, when it is all over,
it will still keep watch

Corollary

my own private Moon

The Moon is also not the Moon
but what all of us think it to be, just
a guess, perhaps
a delusion, a messenger maybe, a wish
that it may all go on forever. And so
that other Moon, the imagined
one, shrine to hopes, the place to dream, the
ever-present sphere open to
all possibilities,
–closer to home, with possibly fewer craters,
a little less vivid maybe–,
is out to get us if we do not pay it
the attention
it deserves: it watches over every instant
of our lifespan
to prove that what counts
is the survival of
those
who can reflect light

- THE END -

Friends of Alice Publishing 2018

ISBN 978-0-9956441-5-1

.

Printed in Poland
by Amazon Fulfillment
Poland Sp. z o.o., Wrocław